The Power Of The Altar

Rebuilding the Altars in Our Churches

Bishop Dr. Roderick G. Senior

ISBN: 978-1-958404-23-2 (paperback)

Printed in the United States of America

Dedication

This book is dedicated to my wonderful, loving, and supportive wife, Cheryl; my wife of thirty years, one who knows the power of the altar and is a true intercessor.

Thank you for the support and love; I really appreciate it.

Love you, dear.

Acknowledgments

All major projects need a great team to help in its undertaking and the success of this book was no different. I am ever appreciative to my friends who laboured extremely hard with me to give birth to this message for the church.

Special thanks to Jenice Forbes, for her tremendous contribution to the content of this book. Her views on the power of the altar were really insightful and powerful.

Finally, God be praised for His leading, guidance, and inspiration towards the content in this book.

God calls us first…not to a platform, but to an altar.
— JD Greear

Table of Contents

Introduction

In studying the patterns of God, the Father, His desire to redeem mankind was a promise. This promise can be deemed as a covenant. However, for a covenant to carry weight, it needs to be supplemented with a sacrifice. In this example, Jesus Christ, the Lamb of God, fulfilled this responsibility. The cross on which He died was symbolic of the altar. Jesus was the *sacrificial Lamb*. The promise was the release of the *Holy Spirit*. However, because spirits respond to altars, Jesus had to pay the price for you and me to receive this wonderful gift of the Holy Spirit.

1 John 5:7-8 highlights this mystery:

*For there are three that bear witness in heaven: the Father, the Word, and the Holy Spirit; and these three are one. And there are three that bear witness on earth: the **Spirit**, the **water**, and the **blood**; and these three agree as one. (NKJV – emphasis mine).*

You will recall in John 19:34 the occurrence of water and blood:

*But one of the soldiers pierced His side with a spear, and immediately **blood** and **water** came out. (NKJV – emphasis mine).*

However, earlier in John 19:30 we see the manifestation of the Spirit:

*So when Jesus had received the sour wine, He said, "It is finished!" And bowing His head, He gave up His **spirit**. (NKJV – emphasis mine).*

The Spirit of Christ was in His blood. That is why it was necessary for Him to have gone to the cross.

***For the life of the flesh is in the blood**, and I have given it to you upon the altar to make atonement for your souls; for it is the blood that makes atonement for the soul. (Leviticus 17:11 – NKJV – emphasis mine).*

With this revelation, it is important to note that the earth itself responds to altars which are established by covenants. These covenants are then serviced by spirits (due to the sacrifices that invite them). Each covenant carries a message and a voice. In the land, for example, they dictate the affairs and mannerisms of men. The land has its own governance and, hence, an individual is not controlled solely by his intellect or consciousness but by the dictates and ways of the land. If they are not obeyed, then the inhabitants will suffer the consequences.

Let us look at the following Scripture:

Then the king of Assyria brought people from Babylon, Cuthah, Ava, Hamath, and from Sepharvaim, and *placed them in the cities of Samaria instead of the children of Israel; and they took possession of Samaria and dwelt in its cities. And it was so, at the beginning of their dwelling there, that **they did not fear the Lord**; therefore the Lord sent lions among them, which killed some of them. So they spoke to the king of Assyria, saying, "The nations whom you have removed and placed in the cities of Samaria do not know **the rituals of the God of the land**; therefore He has sent lions among them, and indeed, they are killing them because they do not know the rituals of the God of the land." Then the king of Assyria commanded, saying, "Send there one of the priests whom you brought from there; let him go and dwell there, **and let him teach them the rituals of the God of the land**." Then one of the priests whom they had carried away from Samaria came and dwelt in Bethel, and taught them how they should fear the Lord. (2 Kings 17:24-28 – NKJV – emphasis mine).*

A corresponding Scripture is found in Isaiah 24:5:

*The **earth** also is defiled under the inhabitants thereof; because they have transgressed the **laws**, changed the **ordinance**, broken the everlasting **covenant**. (KJV – emphasis mine).*

This land of Samaria had precepts which were not followed. As such, not only were the inhabitants rejected, but God caused animals to defend the covenant. The reason for this is because God's covenant with and for a land is not limited to just individuals, but it also extends to creation.

*And in that day will I make a **covenant for them with the beasts** of the field and with **the fowls of heaven**, and with the **creeping things of the ground**: and I will break the bow and the sword and the battle out of the earth, and will make them to lie down safely. (Hosea 2:18 – KJV – emphasis mine).*

*You shall laugh at destruction and famine, and you shall not be afraid of the beasts of the earth. For you shall have **a covenant with the stones of the field, and the beasts of the field. (Job 5:22-23a – NKJV – emphasis mine).***

By establishing a covenant with God and with creation, the earth will reject the decrees of evil men who desire to use the blood of animals to strike us.

Chapter 1
What is the Altar

From examining the life of Abraham, it can be deduced that he had a rich understanding of the ways of the altar, covenant, and sacrifice. An example of this is noted in the scriptures when God promised Abraham that his descendants would possess the land of Canaan. Abraham raised an altar as a memorial to mark the Word of God.

*Then the Lord appeared to Abram and said, "To your descendants I will give this land." And there **he built an altar to the Lord**, who had appeared to him. And he moved from there to the mountain east of Bethel, and he pitched his tent with Bethel on the west and Ai on the east; **there he built an altar** to the Lord and called on the name of the Lord. (Genesis 12:7-8 – NKJV – emphasis mine).*

The word *altar* comes from the Latin word *altarium*, meaning "high," and also the Latin word *adolere*, which means to ritually burn or sacrifice.

The Hebrew word for *altar* is *mizbeah* – "place of slaughter," while the Greek word is *thusiasterion*, – "a place of sacrifice or a place of holocaust."

With the Latin and Hebrew meanings, an altar is a high place of sacrifice where religious ceremonies are done and sacrifices are offered.

An altar was to serve as a means by which the blood of an animal offered in sacrifice might be brought into contact with, or otherwise transferred to, the deity of the worshipper. For this purpose, in the earliest period, a single stone sufficed. Either the blood was poured over this stone, which was regarded as the temporary abode of the deity, or the stone was anointed with part, and the rest poured out at its base.[1]

"An altar is a place of prayer or worship of God or gods. It is a contact place with the spirit or spiritual world. It is a place of discussion, dialogue, and communication with spiritual powers. It is a place of spiritual sacrifice or making of covenants. God blesses His people at the altar of prayer. The foundation for a successful Christian life and ministry is rooted in the altar of prayer. (see Genesis 8:20-22; Genesis 12:6-8; Luke 24:49)"[2]

I would also like to highlight some short definitions of an altar:

> ➢ An altar is where humanity meets divinity.
> ➢ It is a place of divine encounters.
> ➢ It is a place of worship.

---

[1] Hastings Bible Dictionary
[2] Secret Power of Altars by Apostle Simon Gichinga

- ➢ It is a place of sacrifice.
- ➢ An altar is where we encounter the supernatural.
- ➢ It is a structure on which offerings are made to a deity.
- ➢ It is a place designed, separated, and consecrated for worship unto God.
- ➢ It is a gate of transaction between the spiritual and physical.
- ➢ It is a place of divine manifestation, worship, deliverance, and breakthrough; prayers are answered at an altar.

"To the place of the altar which he had made there at first. And there Abram called on the name of the Lord." (Genesis 13:4 - NKJV).

In Genesis 13:18, Abram built another altar, exemplifying that this was a pattern that he followed everywhere he went so the Spirit of God could relate to him on the earth. Spirits (be they godly or ungodly, i.e., angels or demons) have no legal grounds to operate on earth without an altar being raised and a sacrifice being offered. This is why Jesus said the following in John 16:7:

"Nevertheless, I tell you the truth. It is to your advantage that I go away; for if I do not go away, the Helper will not come to you; but if I depart, I will send Him to you." (NKJV).

Chapter 2
A Brief History of Altars in the Bible

For one to fully understand the power of the altar, a history walk must be taken in the scriptures. Let me start by looking at the book of Genesis (The book of beginnings).

Cain And Abel

The first recording of a sacrificial offering at an altar is found in Genesis 4, where Cain and Abel went to offer a sacrifice to God. Cain was a farmer, and Abel was a shepherd; both took of the produce of their occupation to God. God rejected Cain's offering and accepted that of Abel, which led to Cain killing Abel.

A deep study of the book of Genesis also shows that all sacrifices offered were that of an animal and not of the crops from one's field. We can safely conclude that a sacrificial system was instituted by God as an atonement for the sins of man.

It can be interpreted that Cain's sacrifice reflected the state of his heart, which led to him killing his brother.

God looks beyond one's sacrifice and He looks at the heart, for out of the heart comes bitterness and hatred.

"O generation of vipers, how can ye, being evil, speak good things? for out of the abundance of the heart the mouth speaketh." (Matthew 12:34 - KJV).

"But those things which proceed out of the mouth come forth from the heart; and they defile the man." (Matthew 15:18 - KJV).

"For out of the heart proceed evil thoughts, murders, adulteries, fornications, thefts, false witness, blasphemies:" (Matthew 15:19 - KJV).

Noah

The second altar mentioned in the book of Genesis was built by Noah after the flood.

And Noah builded an altar unto the LORD; and took of every clean beast, and of every clean fowl, and offered burnt offerings on the altar. And the LORD smelled a sweet savour; and the LORD said in his heart, I will not again curse the ground any more for man's sake; for the imagination of man's heart is evil from his youth; neither will I again smite any more every thing living, as I have done. While the earth remaineth, seedtime and harvest, and cold and heat, and summer and winter, and day and night shall not cease. (Genesis 8:20-22 - KJV).

After the flood, Noah, being a just and perfect man, built an altar unto the Lord. This was his offering of thanksgiving to God for His mercy and grace. It also served as an atonement offering for man that would open the door for the grace of God to reach man through the ages and secure the salvation of mankind. The power of Noah's sacrifice ensured that God provided salvation for mankind, which was a provision for future generations.

"Sacrifice is an act in which the transgressor slays an animal and offers it in whole, or in part as representative of the whole, to God. In this act he acknowledges his guilt, the claim of the offended law upon his life, and the mercy of the Lord in accepting a substitute to satisfy this claim for the returning penitent. He at the same time actually accepts the mercy of the Most High and comes forward to plead it in the appointed way of reconciliation. The burnt offering is the most perfect symbol of this substitution, and most befitting the present occasion, when life has been granted to the inmates of the ark amidst the universal death."[3]

Noah offered the very best of the animals on the altar. When he lit the wood under the sacrifice, he went into a time of prayer and worship. Prayer and worship mingled with the smoke or sweet soothing aroma of the offering evoked God's response, as a righteous man with a pure heart was crying out to Him. The result of such moved God to make a

---

[3] Barnes notes on the Bible

promise and a pledge never to destroy mankind again by water.

Abraham's Altars

Abraham built several altars unto the Lord. Continuing in the book of Genesis, God dealt with man on a one-to-one basis; therefore, altars had to be erected in different locations unto God. This was man's way of communicating with God through repentance, prayer, worship, and thanksgiving.

Abraham saw the goodness of God in his life, so he constantly gave honour and love at the altar. This was also an example for his seed to follow; hence, Isaac and Jacob became builders of altars, and their descendants also built altars. (see Genesis 12:7-8, Genesis 13:3-4, Genesis 13:18, Genesis 22:9-10, Genesis 26:24-25).

Requirements For The Altar in the Old Testament

*"And **Abraham** took the **wood** of the burnt offering, and laid it upon Isaac his son; and he took the **fire** in his hand, and a **knife**; and they went both of them together. And Isaac spake unto Abraham his father, and said, My father: and he said, Here am I, my son. And he said, Behold the fire and the wood: but where is the **lamb** for a burnt offering? And Abraham said, My son, God will provide himself a lamb for a burnt offering: so they went both of them together. And they came to the place which God had told him of; and Abraham **built an altar** there, and laid the wood in order,*

and bound Isaac his son, and laid him on the altar upon the wood." (Genesis 22:6-9 – KJV – emphasis mine).

A combination of things must happen at the altar for the altar to act or come alive:

— Someone must prepare the altar; the wood must be without insects and must not be rotting.
— The animal that goes on the altar must be alive; the sacrifice must be without blemish.
— Blood must be shed and flow on the altar.
— The wood must be set on fire.
— Worship must take place.

With everything in place, there will be an encounter; the altar will speak. ***Every altar is powerless without a sacrifice.***

Chapter 3
Are Altars Relevant Today

To fully assess this relevance, the following questions can be taken into consideration:

— Do we still need to build altars?
— Do we need a lamb?
— Do we need the high priest to offer up sacrifices for us?

The answer is a resounding **No!** Jesus is now our High Priest and Passover Lamb.

Jesus, Our Passover Lamb

We no longer need wood, animal sacrifice, knife, blood, altar or fire to offer our sacrifices because Jesus has become our sacrificial Lamb. I love the words of this chorus: *"We don't have to slay no lamb anymore. We don't have to place no blood on the door. Someone has taken the place of the lamb and He is the great I AM."*

Jesus is our Passover Lamb. He died for the sins of the world on the cross. His blood was shed and He presented Himself to God as a living sacrifice, holy and without blemish for the sins of mankind.

"But he was wounded for our transgressions, he was bruised for our iniquities: the chastisement of our peace was upon him; and with his stripes we are healed." (Isaiah 53:5 - KJV).

"For even Christ our passover is sacrificed for us:" (1 Corinthians 5:7b - KJV).

John the baptists spoke of Jesus being the Lamb of God:

"The next day John seeth Jesus coming unto him, and saith, Behold the Lamb of God, which taketh away the sin of the world." (John 1:29 - KJV).

As the Lamb of God, Jesus had to be spotless; thus, at His trial, the rulers could find no fault or sin in Him.

Philip declares Him to be the Lamb in Act 8:32:

"The place of the scripture which he read was this, He was led as a sheep to the slaughter; and like a lamb dumb before his shearer, so opened he not his mouth:" (KJV).

Jesus, Our High Priest

Each sacrifice needs a high priest to offer it up; hence, Jesus became our high priest, but not a high priest from the tribe of the Levities. He superseded the Levitical priesthood system. He was not a descendant of Aaron (the first high priest of Israel), but Jesus became a high priest according to the order of Melchizedek, which speaks of His deity. Jesus was fully God, meaning He could not sin. He was fully man, so He could identify with us and bore the pain of the punishment of our sins on the cross.

"If therefore perfection were by the Levitical priesthood, (for under it the people received the law,) what further need was there that another priest should rise after the order of Melchizedek, and not be called after the order of Aaron?" (Hebrews 7:11 - KJV).

"By so much was Jesus made a surety of a better testament. And they truly were many priests, because they were not suffered to continue by reason of death: But this man, because he continueth ever, hath an unchangeable priesthood." (Hebrews 7:22-24 - KJV).

"The author of the letter to the Hebrews writes that there was much to say which was hard to explain regarding Jesus' training to become High Priest, because they had become dull of hearing (see Hebrews 5:11-14). You will discover the deepest mysteries of Jesus' high priestly education in the mystery of Christ "manifested in the flesh, justified in the Spirit, seen by angels" after the resurrection. For just as every high priest taken from among men is appointed for men in things pertaining to God (see Hebrews 5:1), so it was necessary that our heavenly High Priest also be taken from among men. But if someone does not have the flesh and blood of a man, he is not a man. And if he cannot be tempted, he is not a man. But God be praised that we have a High

Priest who was tried in every point—every kind of temptation—yet without sin. In other words, He conquered His own will and the temptations that came from His flesh so completely and perfectly that no sin or blemish was found in Him during the temptation. This cannot always be said about us in our temptations. That is why it is expressly mentioned when referring to Jesus."[4]

The Blood Of Jesus

Jesus shed His blood for the sins of the world. The blood of Jesus is still flowing on our spiritual altars and the blood of Jesus is still speaking on our behalf. We must attest that there is power and victory in the blood of Jesus. Also, the blood of Jesus is a fountain that can never run dry.

"Forasmuch as ye know that ye were not redeemed with corruptible things, as silver and gold, from your vain conversation received by tradition from your fathers; But with the precious blood of Christ, as of a lamb without blemish and without spot:" (1 Peter 1:18-19 - KJV).

Jesus was slain for the sins of the world, and by His blood He redeemed us to God. This redemption is for all people and for all nations of the world.

---

[4] Johan Oscar Smith

The blood of Jesus was shed in seven places to signify the breaking of all curses:

1. Blood from Jesus – His face – Jesus praying in the garden – protecting us from every sorry, depression and oppression of the devil.

2. Blood from Jesus - His back – protects us from every and all darts of the devil and every evil word thrown at us.

3. Blood from Jesus - His head – crown of thorns – protecting our minds from every mind-manipulating demons.

4. Blood from Jesus - His shoulders – weight of the cross – rest assured that all burdens are lifted at calvary.

5. Blood from Jesus – His hands – Jesus is carrying us all the way. Whatever we touch will be blessed.

6. Blood from Jesus - His feet - Psalm 23:4 says *"Yea, though I walk through the valley of the shadow of death, I will fear no evil: for thou art with me; thy rod and thy staff they comfort me." (KJV)*.

7. Blood from Jesus - His side – Jesus is always beside us, never leaving us – our Protector.

Here is a list of the benefits of the blood of Jesus according to Kenneth Copeland:

1. **Redemption Through the Blood of Jesus.** "...we have redemption through His blood..." (Ephesians 1:7 - NKJV).

2. **Fellowship With God Through the Blood of Jesus.** "...having boldness to enter the Holiest by the blood of Jesus." (Hebrews 10:19 - NKJV).

3. **Healing Through the Blood of Jesus.** "...by His stripes we are healed." (Isaiah 53:5 - NKJV).

4. **Protection Through the Blood of Jesus.** "...when I see the blood, I will pass over you..." (Exodus 12:13 - KJV).

5. **Authority Over the Devil Through the Blood of Jesus.** "And they overcame him by the blood of the Lamb, and by the word of their testimony." (Revelation 12:11a - KJV).

"The curse is death, sin, sickness, disease, poverty, lack, depression—anything bad you can think of. Adam's treason gave Satan authority over the life of man, but because of the power of the blood of Jesus, the moment you made Jesus Christ the Lord of your life, you were **redeemed** from the curse and **Satan was put out of business.**"[5]

---

[5] Kenneth Copeland

Sacrifice

The Lamb of God paid the ultimate price as a sacrifice, and as a result, we are no longer bound by the law to offer animals as sacrifices. However, sacrificial offerings are not obsolete. The question then is, "What is a sacrifice?" A sacrifice, as the word suggests, is anything that will cost you (from your resources to your time). Jesus was truly a sacrifice for mankind because He was the *only* begotten Son of the heavenly Father. A good example of a sacrifice is your money, but what qualifies money to be a sacrifice?

You will recall that in Genesis 3:19, God said *"By the sweat of your brow you will eat your food." (NIV)*. Labour is often rewarded with money, and this money is earned by sweat. Scientifically, there is a correlation between sweat and blood, given that capillary blood vessels feed the sweat glands. Thus, we can say then that not only is money connected to our sweat but also to our blood. Therefore, because there is blood, then a sacrifice must be involved.

Hence, our giving to the Lord should not be with the attitude that God needs our money (seeing that the street of New Jerusalem is made up of gold) but rather with the understanding that the whole world sits on the sacrifice of the Lamb's blood.

Furthermore, a sacrifice can also be anything that you deny yourself for the sake of the Lord. That is why Romans 12:1 admonishes us to *"present your **bodies a living sacrifice**,* *holy, acceptable unto God, which is your reasonable service."* (KJV – emphasis mine). In not conforming to the things of the world as commanded in Romans 12:2, that is also a sacrifice because you are denying yourself of worldly pleasures.

Sacrifices And Covenants

Sacrifices and covenants are necessary because they are the currency by which we trade in life. These are the keys that open the gates for spirits to walk with you on the earth. Jacob possessed this understanding. In Genesis 28, Jacob followed the patterns of his grandfather by raising an altar upon the visitation of the Lord after he made a vow (see Genesis 28:20-22). By this, the angel of the Lord had access to visit him as evidenced in Genesis 31:11-13:

*Then the Angel of God spoke to me in a dream, saying, 'Jacob.' And I said, 'Here I am.' I am the God of Bethel, **where you anointed the pillar and where you made a vow to Me**. Now arise, get out of this land, and return to the land of your family.'"* (NKJV – emphasis mine).

Thus, when you make a covenant, it justifies angels to walk with you because they are enforcers of the covenant as shown in the below Scriptures:

*Bless the Lord, **you His angels**, who excel in strength, **who do His word**, heeding the voice of His word.* (Psalm 103:20 – NKJV – emphasis mine).

*Are not the **angels all ministering spirits (servants) sent out in the service [of God for the assistance]** of those who are to inherit salvation? (Hebrews 1:14 – AMPC – emphasis mine).*

Jacob understood that his promise/vow/covenant to the Lord had to be substantiated by a sacrifice in order for the covenant to be supervised by angels. Consider the below Scripture:

***Take with you words**, and turn to the Lord: say unto him, Take away all iniquity, and receive us graciously: so will we **render the calves of our lips**. (Hosea 14:2 – KJV – emphasis mine).*

This Scripture illustrates that our words should be supported by a sacrifice. Though we are no longer bound to use bullocks and bulls as sacrificial offerings, the Lord expects us to follow His pattern through giving. Your gifts and sacrifices attract spirits, and they are needful in order to complete your request.

*Be careful for nothing; but in every thing by prayer and supplication **with thanksgiving** let your requests be made known unto God. (Philippians 4:6 – KJV – emphasis mine).*

Our requests should not stop with mere words but should be completed with a sacrifice. This is what the Father did, i.e. He paid for our salvation from the grip of Satan by a sacrifice: His only Son.

33

As established, the covenant is a promise or a vow. It acts as an "I swear." For example, God made a covenant with David of which the sun, moon, and stars are all witnesses.

*"Thus says the Lord: 'If **My covenant** is not with **day** and **night**, and if I have not appointed **the ordinances of heaven and earth**, then I will cast away the descendants of Jacob and David My servant, so that I will not take any of his descendants to be rulers over the descendants of Abraham, Isaac, and Jacob. For I will cause their captives to return, and will have mercy on them.'" (Jeremiah 33:25-26 – NKJV – emphasis mine).*

It is by your covenant that God hands over inheritance to you as was in the days of Abraham. Similarly, by covenant, you pull down the hand of the invisible (i.e., the angelic) to deliver to you what you desire, as was in the days of Jacob when he wrestled with the angel all night (see Genesis 32:24-30). Your covenant therefore acts as a medium for a transaction and gives you the assurance that God will hear your prayers. As such, it is imperative that your covenants with the Lord concerning your life, family, business, health, and everything else are renewed regularly.

The natural mirrors the spiritual. Marital vows are renewable and, likewise, this should be applied to our love relationship with the Lord Jesus. This is one of the reasons for partaking in the Lord's supper. We do this to renew our vows to love Him with all our hearts, souls, and strength (see 1 Corinthians 11:24-25). Hence, the altars of righteousness raised unto the Lord, regardless of their purpose, must be revisited from time to time.

Chapter 4
Christian Altar Today

As Christians, our altars can be in our homes; by our bedside, living room or that secret place in our homes. It can be at church, where our posture is either kneeling, standing, or sitting. It is our place of worship and prayer to God, our place of encounter with God—where His presence fills our space with awe and glory. It is that place that is pregnant with the glory of God, the full weight of God's presence; nothing holding back all of God's glory, majesty, and splendor.

Our altar is where we see ourselves—how unworthy we are. We come in repentance, we crucify the flesh, we die daily, and we become more like Christ. At the altar, deliverance must take place, healing must happen, and one must walk into their breakthrough. Victory for a believer is in the Word of God. Heaven shows up at your altar with all power and might.

"I protest by your rejoicing which I have in Christ Jesus our Lord, I die daily." (1 Corinthians 15:31 - KJV).

"The Spirit of the Lord is upon me, because he hath anointed me to preach the gospel to the poor; he hath sent me to heal the brokenhearted, to preach deliverance to the captives,

and recovering of sight to the blind, to set at liberty them that are bruised, to preach the acceptable year of the Lord." (Luke 4:18-19 - KJV).

Principalities and powers are defeated at your altar. Why worry and fear the power of darkness when Jesus won that victory for us? We must walk in that victory on the earth. The gates of hell, the authority of hell, powers and the schemes of hell cannot prevail against us; they will come at us, but they will never overpower us while we stay at the altar.

"And I say also unto thee, That thou art Peter, and upon this rock I will build my church; and the gates of hell shall not prevail against it. And I will give unto thee the keys of the kingdom of heaven: and whatsoever thou shalt bind on earth shall be bound in heaven: and whatsoever thou shalt loose on earth shall be loosed in heaven." (Matthew 16:18-19 - KJV).

"And having spoiled principalities and powers, he made a shew of them openly, triumphing over them in it." (Colossians 2:15 - KJV).

The praise and worship of a believer at the altar will silence the powers of the underworld. Our praise is not normal; when we praise and worship God at the altar, He comes and sits in our praise. His presence is felt and, at times, seen.

"Let the high praises of God be in their mouth, and a two-edged sword in their hand; To execute vengeance upon the heathen, and punishments upon the people; To bind their kings with chains, and their nobles with fetters of iron; To execute upon them the judgment written: this honour have all his saints. Praise ye the Lord." (Psalm 149:6-9 - KJV).

Establish that covenant with God at the altar. Get your Bible, read that promise for your life, and make it a covenant between you and God. Let it become a perpetual covenant; the Lord will honour His Word.

Is there something in your life that you need to remind God about by His Word; then go ahead and remind Him, but make it a covenant.

"I will worship toward thy holy temple, and praise thy name for thy lovingkindness and for thy truth: for thou hast magnified thy word above all thy name." (Psalm 138:2 - KJV).

Chapter 5
Members of Our Bodies as Altars

We have established that an altar is a place of communion between God and man. In 1 Corinthians 6:19-20, not only do we see that our bodies are the indwelling of the Holy Spirit, but we are admonished to keep our bodies pure. Furthermore, our bodies, being the altar of God, were purchased by the *Lamb's blood.*

*"What? Know ye not **that your body is the temple of the Holy Ghost** which is in you, which ye have of God, and ye are not your own? For ye are **bought with a price**: therefore glorify God in your body, and in your spirit, which are God's." (1 Corinthians 6:19-20 – KJV – emphasis mine).*

The body houses the heart, and the heart is the altar of God's visitation. In Genesis 6:9, we see Noah who was a *"...just and righteous man, blameless in his [evil] generation; Noah walked [in habitual fellowship] with God." (AMPC).* Thus, God delighted in him because *"...Noah found grace in the eyes of the Lord." (Genesis 6:8 - KJV).* In having a right heart posture, Noah enjoyed communion with the Lord and also touched the heart of God.

*"And Noah builded an **altar** unto the Lord; and took of every clean beast, and of every clean fowl, and offered burnt offerings on the **altar**. And the Lord smelled a sweet savour; and the Lord said in his **heart**, I will not again curse the ground any more for man's sake; for the imagination of man's heart is evil from his youth; neither will I again smite any more every thing living, as I have done." (Genesis 8:20-21 – KJV – emphasis mine).*

The altar became a connecting point between man and God. Furthermore, the acceptable sacrifice offered was the incentive that attracted the blessings of God. Not only was Noah's life acceptable, but his sacrifice was accepted. By this, we can conclude that there is a blessing that comes with righteous and holy living.

The Tongue As An Altar

"Death and life are in the power of the tongue, *and those who love it will eat its fruit." (Proverbs 18:21 – NKJV – emphasis mine).*

Scripture enlightens us with the knowledge that there is an altar in our tongues called death and life. However, though we have been given authority to decree things so they can be established (see Job 22:28), we are often careless about what we say, which then leaves us bewildered as to why our lives are the way they are. The tongue plays a vital role in God's prophetic agenda. It is the medium through which God establishes His will on the earth.

Before Jeremiah's commission, God touched his mouth and placed His words in his mouth (see Jeremiah 1:9). Similarly, in wanting to create new heavens and a new earth for the city of Jerusalem, He first put His Word in the mouths of His people (see Isaiah 51:16).

We were created in the image and likeness of God, making us gods (see Genesis 1:26 and Psalm 82:6). Thus, the boldness that we have to wield this authority is patterned by the Son of God. Isaiah 11:4 sheds light on this truth by saying that Christ Jesus will "strike the earth with the **rod of His mouth**, and with the breath of His lips He shall slay the wicked." (NKJV – emphasis mine). Likewise, in both Hebrews 4:12 and Revelation 19:15, we note that the words of His mouth, which are released from His tongue, are likened to a sharp sword.

Every altar carries fire, as seen in Leviticus 6:12-13, where "the fire on the altar shall be kept burning on it; … it shall never go out." (NKJV). To further the point that the tongue is an altar, God decreed that His Word is like fire (see Jeremiah 23:29). Fire is an instrument of judgment. Hence, in Ezekiel 21:2, when God instructed the prophet to drop his word, He was in essence telling him to invoke the judgment of God on the land of Israel.

The Womb As An Altar

An altar acts as a house where covenants are established and spirits are trapped. In examining the womb, three things are present: water, blood, and spirit (the life of the baby). This was the revelation that Hannah had. Though Samuel was unborn in her womb, she vowed to the Lord, i.e., she made a covenant that the child would be for the Lord's service.

*"Then **she made a vow** and said, "O Lord of hosts, if You will indeed look on the affliction of Your maidservant and remember me, and not forget Your maidservant, but will give Your maidservant a male child, **then I will give him to the Lord all the days of his life**, and no razor shall come upon his head." (1 Samuel 1:11 – NKJV – emphasis mine).*

Granted that the earth is referred to as a *she* (see Revelation 12:16), we can infer that the earth also has a womb. Additionally, the womb is a place where both life (birth) and death (miscarriage) take place. Consider therefore why Moses commanded the earth to swallow Korah, Dathan and Abiram (see Numbers 16:28-33). This revelation was discovered from the beginning of time; man was created from the dust (which is from the earth), and he will return to the dust, i.e., the earth which acts as a graveyard (see Genesis 2:7; 3:19).

However, the earth is not the only creation that possesses a womb, but so does the morning:

*Thy people shall be willing in the day of thy power, in the beauties of holiness from the **womb of the morning**: thou hast the **dew** of thy youth. (Psalm 110:3 – KJV – emphasis mine).*

The above Scripture underscores that the early hours of the morning serve as the womb of the day. This is the hours from 3 AM to 6 AM (the 4th watch—see Matthew 14:25), and it is marked by intense spiritual warfare and the activity of spirits. With this insight, this is an opportune time to pray and command the judgment of death on the things that ought not to be and to call forth that which is not as though they are (see Romans 4:17).

*"Give them, O Lord—What will You give? Give them a **miscarrying womb** and **dry breasts!**" (Hosea 9:14 – NKJV – emphasis mine).*

The above Scripture points out that another aspect of the female human body that also serves as an altar is the breasts. The caution to ladies therefore is to be careful who you expose your stomach and breasts to.

The Female Reproductive Organ As An Altar

Given that one's body is the temple of the Lord, then the sexual organ is an altar. In an effort to emphasize the need to keep it holy, Paul warned in 1 Corinthians 6:18 to *"Flee sexual immorality. Every sin that a man does is outside the body, but he who commits **sexual immorality sins against his own body**."* (NKJV – emphasis mine). With this revelation, we understand therefore that the female's private part is also an altar. Hence, it is of utmost importance that you are wary of who you sleep with. This is why God desires that sex is done within the confines of marriage. The reproductive organ of a woman is in the similitude of the temple. There is an outer court, inner court, and holy of holies. The holy of holies (otherwise known as the *most holy place*) of the holy temple is demarcated by a veil (see Hebrews 9:3; Exodus 26:31; Leviticus 16:2).

The term *veil* is associated with the word *hymn* which is a derivative of the word *hymen.* A hymn denotes worship unto the Lord, and it is a sacred act. As such, Aaron, though a high priest, was admonished not to treat the most holy place as common by entering whenever he chooses (see Leviticus 16:2). In like manner, the veil (or hymen) of a woman is considered sacred and must not be broken by anyone except her high priest: her husband.

*I am jealous for you with a godly jealousy. I promised you to one **husband**, to Christ, so that I might present you as a **pure virgin to him**. (2 Corinthians 11:2 – NIV – emphasis mine).*

Jesus Christ, our High Priest (see Hebrews 4:14) was *qualified* to go beyond the veil, which is why it rent in two when He was on the cross.

*Jesus, when he had cried again with a loud voice, yielded up the ghost. And, behold, **the veil of the temple was rent in twain** from the top to the bottom; and the earth did quake, and the rocks rent. (Matthew 27:50-51 – KJV – emphasis mine).*

Chapter 6
Three Types Of Altars

1. Personal
2. Family
3. Corporate

Personal Altar

A personal altar involves you and God alone. It is our quiet time with God; our closet encounter with God when we shut out the noise and enter into that secret place with God.

"But thou, when thou prayest, enter into thy closet, and when thou hast shut thy door, pray to thy Father which is in secret; and thy Father which seeth in secret shall reward thee openly." (Matthew 6:6 - KJV).

Examples Of Personal Altars

Jabez built his personal altar and went in unto God, and he called unto God.

"And Jabez was more honourable than his brethren: and his mother called his name Jabez, saying, Because I bare him with sorrow. And Jabez called on the God of Israel, saying, Oh that thou wouldest bless me indeed, and enlarge my

coast, and that thine hand might be with me, and that thou wouldest keep me from evil, that it may not grieve me! And God granted him that which he requested." (1 Chronicles 4:9-10 - KJV).

Jabez asked God for four things:

1. **Bless me indeed.** The blessing of God is real and brings real effects; those whom God blesses are blessed.

2. **Enlarge my coast.** The increase of assets, houses, lands, animals, business, wealth.

3. **Thine hand might be with me.** Hands speak of covering and protection from evil.

4. **Keep me from evil, that it may not grieve me.** Evil is real, and Jabez didn't want evil to afflict and destroy him.

At Jabez's personal altar, he cried unto God, and he received all that he asked for. The curse he had walked around with and lived with was now broken totally and completely.

Our personal altar must not only be a cry for self alone, but as we pray to God, we pray for our family, nations, and others. As we look in our nation and see what is happening—we see the poverty, crime, government, and economy—we must put these and others before the Lord for His divine intervention. Our personal altar must be a place of deep travailing and intercession.

We must intercede so we can live a peaceful life on this earth. Christ died for the sins of the world, and it is His desire for all to be saved. Our intercession will enable us to accomplish this goal. This point is made clear by Paul's letter to Timothy:

"I exhort therefore, that, first of all, supplications, prayers, intercessions, *and* giving of thanks, be made for all men; For kings, and *for* all that are in authority; that we may lead a quiet and peaceable life in all godliness and honesty. For this *is* good and acceptable in the sight of God our Saviour; Who will have all men to be saved, and to come unto the knowledge of the truth. For *there is* one God, and one mediator between God and men, the man Christ Jesus;" (1 Timothy 2:1-5 – KJV – emphasis mine).

King David also erected a personal altar unto the Lord, which stopped the judgment of God towards the nation. He had done a census, looking to his own strength and not to God. His heart smote him, and he knew he had sinned, and for this, there was a punishment.

"Go and say unto David, Thus saith the LORD, I offer thee three things; choose thee one of them, that I may do it unto thee. So Gad came to David, and told him, and said unto him, Shall seven years of famine come unto thee in thy land? or wilt thou flee three months before thine enemies, while they pursue thee? or that there be three days' pestilence in thy land? now advise, and see what answer I shall return to him that sent me. And David said unto Gad, I am in a great

strait: let us fall now into the hand of the LORD; for his mercies are great: and let me not fall into the hand of man."
(2 Samuel 24:12-14 - KJV).

David had to raise an altar. The owner wanted to give David the threshing floor for free, but he refused. There must be a cost to get into the presence of the Lord as we cry for the land and for God to hold back His judgment over the land.

"And Araunah said, Wherefore is my lord the king come to his servant? And David said, To buy the threshingfloor of thee, to build an altar unto the LORD, that the plague may be stayed from the people. And Araunah said unto David, Let my lord the king take and offer up what seemeth good unto him: behold, here be oxen for burnt sacrifice, and threshing instruments and other instruments of the oxen for wood. All these things did Araunah, as a king, give unto the king. And Araunah said unto the king, The LORD thy God accept thee. And the king said unto Araunah, Nay; but I will surely buy it of thee at a price: neither will I offer burnt offerings unto the LORD my God of that which doth cost me nothing. So David bought the threshingfloor and the oxen for fifty shekels of silver. And David built there an altar unto the LORD, and offered burnt offerings and peace offerings. So the LORD was intreated for the land, and the plague was stayed from Israel." (2 Samuel 24:21-25 - KJV).

I firmly believe that it is the prayer of the church, both individually and corporately, that is saving the world and withholding the judgment of God from the earth.

Family Altar

A family is a group of people living together in the same home. The family provides its members with:

— Protection
— Companionship
— Security
— Socialization

Do you have a family altar? Are you taking care of your family altar? It is important that all families have a family altar.

Who is taking care of your family altar? Is it being serviced with prayer and fasting? Unless we ensure that our family altar is serviced and attended to, we cannot experience the covering and protection of God.

It is not to be ignored but we must investigate our family lineage as there are families operating under a curse. Such curse/curses must be broken at the righteous family altar in order for the blessings of God to flow in the family.

When we think of a curse, we are thinking of evil, mischief, injury, and spells operating in the family that must be broken.

Jacob Raised An Altar For His Family

After spending twenty years at Laban's house, God told Jacob to go home and face Esau, his brother, who had vowed to kill him because Jacob had used trickery to get the blessings of the firstborn from Isaac, his father, and this could not be reversed (see Genesis 27).

On his way home, he heard that Esau was coming with over four hundred men to slay him and his family, but Jacob raised an altar and went to God for his family.

"Deliver me, I pray thee, from the hand of my brother, from the hand of Esau: for I fear him, lest he will come and smite me, and the mother with the children." (Genesis 32:11 - KJV).

That same night Jacob had an encounter with an angel, and he wrestled with the angel all night until he got his breakthrough, but it came with great pain. He was crippled after that encounter.

"And he said, Let me go, for the day breaketh. And he said, I will not let thee go, except thou bless me. And he said unto him, what is thy name? And he said, Jacob. And he said, thy name shall be called no more Jacob, but Israel: for as a prince hast thou power with God and with men, and hast prevailed. And Jacob asked him, and said, tell me, I pray thee, thy name. And he said, wherefore is it that thou dost ask after my name? And he blessed him there. And Jacob

called the name of the place Peniel: for I have seen God face to face, and my life is preserved." (Genesis 32:26-30 - KJV).

Instead of Esau killing him, he had no other choice but to hug him.

David paid a price for the threshing floor; Jacob paid the price for his personal deliverance and the deliverance of his family. What is the price we are paying for ourselves, our family, and the nation at our altars? Are we travailing earnestly or do we just say a quick prayer? There is a cost for breakthrough and deliverance; it takes deep travailing and intercession for us to receive freedom in some areas of our lives and enter in our godly purpose and destiny.

Like Elijah, let us repair the broken, individual altars and restart with a repaired altar. God is waiting to send the fire from heaven on our altars; this fire speaks of deliverance and breakthrough and an unforgettable life-changing encounter with God. Great change will be wrought in our lives by the power and presence of the Lord.

"Thou wilt shew me the path of life: in thy presence is fulness of joy; at thy right hand there are pleasures for evermore." (Psalm 16:11 - KJV).

Gideon had to destroy his family altar and build an altar unto God before he could go to war and be victorious in the battle.

"And it came to pass the same night, that the LORD said unto him, Take thy father's young bullock, even the second bullock of seven years old, and throw down the altar of Baal that thy father hath, and cut down the grove that is by it: And build an altar unto the LORD thy God upon the top of this rock, in the ordered place, and take the second bullock, and offer a burnt sacrifice with the wood of the grove which thou shalt cut down." (Judges 6:25-26 - KJV).

Once we keep our family altar alive with the fire of prayer, all other evil altars in the family will be demolished, cease to operate, lose their power and crumble at your altar.

Prayer is the breath that gives life to a family home, and when a family prays together, the following happens:

a) God is glorified.
b) Protection comes over the family.
c) Respect and love flow in the home.
d) Godly fear fills the heart of the family.
e) Deliverance takes place.
f) Hope resides in the heart of the family, even in hard times.
g) The family is more united.

"Train up a child in the way he should go: and when he is old, he will not depart from it." (Proverbs 22:6 - KJV).

"And, ye fathers, provoke not your children to wrath: but bring them up in the nurture and admonition of the Lord." (Ephesians 6:4 - KJV).

If we examine Job's life, it exemplifies how our family altar should operate. Job's family altar never died; it was always active. Job knew his role as the priest of his home, the one who must take his family to the altar. He never allowed the fire to go out on his family altar. He kept a close watch on his adult children.

Parents, our children will always be our children, even when they are married and move away from home, so never stop interceding for them at the altar, even when they cannot be present for the prayer meetings.

*"So it was, when the days of feasting had run their course, that Job would send and sanctify them, and he would rise **early in the morning** and offer **burnt offerings** according to the number of them all. For Job said, "It may be that my sons have sinned and cursed God in their hearts." Thus Job did regularly." (Job 1:5 – NKJV – emphasis mine).*

To offer burnt offerings, there had to be an altar to execute these prayers. During the early hours of the morning, not only was Job reminding God of the covenant of life and mercies which were made over his children, but he was renewing the covenants.

Joshua was another man of the spirit who raised an altar in his household by declaring that *"**as for me and my house,** we will serve the Lord"* (Joshua 24:15 – NKJV – emphasis mine). With the understanding that the loins function as a place of covenant, Joshua would have commanded his children to walk in the ways of the Lord while they were yet in his loins.

Similarly, Abraham established an altar of righteousness over his household, so much so that the Lord testified of him.

*"For I know him, that **he will command his children and his household** after him, and **they shall keep the way of the Lord**, to do justice and judgment; that the Lord may bring upon Abraham that which he hath spoken of him."* (Genesis 18:19 – KJV – emphasis mine).

God boasted about Abraham because this covenant was already settled in Genesis 15, long before Abraham's descendants were born. By this observation it can be concluded that the covenant of the family you are born in can either frustrate you or work in your favour. As such, a man must be very careful who he is intimate with because his loins carry a covenant.

Hebrews 7 gives the account that Levi, while yet unborn, paid tithes while in the loins of his father, Abraham.

"For this Melchizedek, king of Salem, priest of the Most High God, who met Abraham returning from the slaughter

*of the kings and blessed him, to whom also **Abraham gave a tenth part of all**, first being translated "king of righteousness," and then also King of Salem, meaning "King of Peace," without father, without mother, without genealogy, having neither beginning of days nor end of life, but made like the Son of God, remains a priest continually. Now consider how great this man was, to whom even the patriarch Abraham gave a tenth of the spoils. And indeed those who are of the **sons of Levi**, who receive the priesthood, have a commandment to receive tithes from the people according to the law, that is, from their brethren, though they have come from the loins of Abraham; but he whose genealogy is not derived from them received tithes from Abraham and blessed him who had the promises. Now beyond all contradiction the lesser is blessed by the better. Here mortal men receive tithes, but there he receives them, of whom it is witnessed that he lives. **Even Levi, who receives tithes, paid tithes through Abraham**, so to speak, for he was **still in the loins of his father** when Melchizedek met him." (Hebrews 7:1-10 – NKJV – emphasis mine).*

By this act, the sons of Levi were so blessed that God Himself was their inheritance (see Deuteronomy 10:9; 18:1). On the contrary, children can inherit curses from their fathers because of the evil altars that were erected and, subsequently, the evil covenants that they were born under. There are certain signs that can serve as warnings that there is a strange covenant speaking in your bloodline against you.

The following list is not exhaustive, but it includes a number of issues that are quite common:

— barrenness in the family.
— children being born out of wedlock.
— premature death.
— high school/college dropouts.
— divorce.
— cycles of poverty or inability to settle in a job.
— chronic diseases and/or mental sicknesses.
— drunkenness.

If you notice any of these patterns, begin to stand in the gap for your family by entering into a time of fasting to break the cycle. Based on revelation, ask the Lord to destroy every evil altar risen against you and your family, whether it is in the heavens, on the earth or underneath the earth using Philippians 2:10. Ask Him to shake the heavens and earth on your behalf using Hebrews 12:26-27. Ask Him to go through your bloodline and sever you from every witchcraft speaking against you from the loins, wombs, and breasts of your ancestors.

From Scripture, we know that though Abraham passed on to glory, his son, Levi, was still being blessed. By this, ask the Lord to silence the evil that is crying out against you from the bones of your ancestors using Job 20:11. Invoke the power of the cross and judge every evil record and handwriting written against you and yours using Colossians 2:14-15 and Isaiah 10:1. Ask the Lord to let His blood speak against every strange blood crying out for evil against you using Revelation 12:11 and Hebrews 12:24. Be very intentional to gather scriptures (see Hosea 14:2) to supplement your prayers because the Word of God cannot be denied (see Psalm 138:2 and Psalm 89:34).

After you have done all the dismantling (see Jeremiah 1:10), be deliberate in raising an altar of righteousness and life over yourself and your family. Be reminded that there is an altar of fire in your tongue of which you can connect to the altar of fire in heaven (see Revelation 8:3). Search the scriptures and pull down the will of God that is written concerning you as preordained in the heaven so it can be manifested here on earth (see Matthew 6:10). Ask the Lord to release His angel to gather fire and scatter it on your behalf (see Revelation 3:5 and Ezekiel 10:2) against every altar of witchcraft.

Corporate Altar

Corporate prayer will:

    a) increase our trust in and dependence on each other.
    b) increase our faith in God.
    c) unifie the body of Christ.
    d) bring edification to the church.
    e) facilitate a greater bonding among believers.

Jesus is always present in our prayer:

"For where two or three are gathered together in my name, there am I in the midst of them." (Matthew 18:20 - KJV).

The altar at your church must always be open for Godly encounters, repentance, renewal, salvation, baptism in the Holy Ghost, refreshing, meeting of needs, deliverance, and breakthrough in one's life, and it must be a time of personal ministry.

There is a call from God for kneeling to take place once again at the altar; get back those kneeling pads and let the people kneel in reverence and submission to God.

In Acts of the apostles, we see corporate altars in the upper room for ten days before Pentecost. They were praying and offering worship unto God and look at the outcome on the Day of Pentecost; the Holy Ghost came.

"These all continued with one accord in prayer and supplication, with the women, and Mary the mother of Jesus, and with his brethren." (Acts 1:14 - KJV).

Another illustration of corporate prayer is when Peter was in prison. The church prayed and he was delivered from prison by an angel:

"Peter therefore was kept in prison: but prayer was made without ceasing of the church unto God for him." (Acts 12:5 - KJV).

"And, behold, the angel of the Lord came upon him, and a light shined in the prison: and he smote Peter on the side,

and raised him up, saying, Arise up quickly. And his chains fell off from his hands." (Acts 12:7 - KJV).

Prayer

What fuels our altars or keeps it going? It is our prayer! Our prayer is the incense, the smoke, the sweet aroma that will bring the presence of God into our midst.

Prayer is communication with God and, since communication is a two process, we need to await God's response to us.

Prayer allows us to come in agreement with the Word of God, so when we talk to God, we use His Word, for the Lord honours His Word.

Prayer is man coming in contact with God, and God coming in contact with man. It is this flow from man to God and God to man, so man should not just talk and get up and leave his altar. He must also wait on God to talk to him at the altar; man must learn to listen.

So many times we do all the talking and don't listen. If you don't listen for God's response, your prayer is incomplete. In prayer, man is touching God, and God is touching man. Man is uniting with God and God is uniting with man; man is in God's presence, and God is in the presence of man.

In praying, man comes before God in humility, with worship, thanksgiving and supplication, and God shows up in His glory, majesty, and power, speaking and uplifting man, causing man to see himself and totally submit to the supreme Creator of the heavens and the earth. Do not rise from your altar until God shows up and speaks to you, until you feel His presence and His glory surrounding you.

At the altar, mourning turns to joy, depression turns to hope, barrenness turns to productivity, curses turn to blessings, and life is transform into the image and likeness of Jesus Christ.

"Prayer is not just man contacting God; it is the mutual contact between man and God. This matter of the contact between God and man is a very great subject in the Bible. We have often said that the purpose of man's living is to be God's vessel. In the universe, God is man's content, and man is God's container. Without man, God has no place to put Himself—He becomes a homeless God. I do not understand why this is so, but I know that it is a fact. In the universe God's greatest need is man. God as an entity in Himself is complete, but as far as His operation in the universe is concerned, He still needs man to fulfill that operation.

By this you can understand the last sentence of Ephesians 1, which says that the church is the Body of Christ, the fullness of Christ. The term fullness is very hard to translate. It not only denotes the fullness of Christ, but also implies the completeness of Christ. Hence, the church is, on the one hand, the fullness of Christ, and on the other hand, the completeness of Christ. In other words, without the church, it seems that Christ is not at all complete.

We all must be very careful in understanding this word, for it can stir up vehement arguments in theology. I do not mean that God is incomplete and that He needs man to make Him complete. What I mean is that God in Himself is perfectly complete, but without man He is not complete in the universe according to His plan. Oh, brothers and sisters, this matter is too glorious."[6]

The fire of prayer at our altar cannot be allowed to go out. We must constantly and daily keep on pouring the fuel of prayer on the altar. Imagine being at home and there is a power outage. If the light goes out in the night, your home will be in darkness. You will have to search and feel around to make sure you do not hit any of the furniture. Darkness brings fear. When the light returns, the darkness disappears; so it is with our altar of prayer. Prayer keeps the darkness away. Prayer pushes back the wiles of the devil, exposes the scheme of Satan and brings salvation and hope to a lost world.

"Rejoice evermore. Pray without ceasing. In everything give thanks: for this is the will of God in Christ Jesus concerning you." (1 Thessalonians 5:16-18 - KJV).

---

[6] Lessons On Prayer By Witness Lee

"Therefore I say unto you, What things soever ye desire, when ye pray, believe that ye receive them, and ye shall have them." (Mark 11:24 - KJV).

"Call unto me, and I will answer thee, and show thee great and mighty things, which thou knowest not." (Jeremiah 33:3 - KJV).

"Prayer at the altar allows you to go into the throne room of God and receive divine revelation and impartation from God, what God has on His mind, and download it on the earth through intercession."[7]

Let your altar speak to you. Do not walk away before your altar speaks. Get that encounter from God at your altar before you walk away. Remember, God created us to have a relationship with Him. He wants to hear us; He wants us to have a personal and intimate relationship with Him, and it is at the altar where such a relationship is developed and fostered.

Here are examples we should follow in keeping our altar:

> ➤ David never left the altar until the plague stopped. *"...David built there an altar unto the LORD, and offered burnt offerings and peace offerings. So the LORD was intreated for the land, and the plague was stayed from Israel." (2 Samuel 24:25 - KJV).*

---

[7] William Duncan

➢ Elijah rebuilt the altar and never walked away from the altar until fire came down from heaven. *"Hear me, O LORD, hear me, that this people may know that thou art the LORD God, and that thou hast turned their heart back again. Then the fire of the LORD fell, and consumed the burnt sacrifice, and the wood, and the stones, and the dust, and licked up the water that was in the trench." (1 Kings 18:37-38 - KJV).*

➢ Jacob never left the altar until he was transformed. The curse of being called *Jacob* was broken and a blessing and name change was given to him. *"And he said, thy name shall be called no more Jacob, but Israel: for as a prince hast thou power with God and with men, and hast prevailed." (Genesis 32:28 - KJV).*

➢ Solomon never stopped praying until fire came down from heaven. This fire represented the presence and glory of God among the people, and the acceptance of the sacrifice. *"Now when Solomon had made an end of praying, the fire came down from heaven, and consumed the burnt offering and the sacrifices; and the glory of the LORD filled the house." (2 Chronicles 7:1 - KJV).*

➢ Daniel never left his altar, even when the decree was signed by the king that would lead to the death of anyone calling on God for a period. He serviced his altar three times a day with his windows open towards Jerusalem. They could see and hear him praying, and this led to an angel coming and shutting the mouths of the lions. *"Then these men assembled, and found Daniel praying and making supplication before his God." (Daniel 6:11 - KJV). "My God hath sent his angel, and hath shut the lions' mouths, that they have not hurt me: forasmuch as before him innocency was found in me; and also before thee, O king, have I done no hurt." (Daniel 6:22 - KJV).*

➢ The disciples gathered in the upper room and, while servicing the altar in prayer and worship, the Holy Ghost fire fell on the early church there. *"These all continued with one accord in prayer and supplication, with the women, and Mary the mother of Jesus, and with his brethren." (Acts 1:14 - KJV).*

Let God show up at your altar. He has made all the preparation in sending His Son, Jesus, into the world to be the perfect sacrifice. He wants to speak to us at our altars. Do not turn Him away. Let Him come in all His glory and power at your altar of prayer.

Chapter 7
The Covenant Of Ancestors

1 John 5:8 gives us insight that blood is a witness, and as a witness, it testifies of either the blessings or the curses owing to a man. We noted earlier that Abraham's descendants were blessed because of the covenant written in his bloodline. Hence, Isaac and Jacob (along with Levi) were rightful inheritors of the promise.

*"Be ye mindful always of his **covenant**; the word which he commanded to a **thousand generations**; Even of the **covenant which he made with Abraham**, and of **his oath unto Isaac**; And hath **confirmed the same to Jacob** for a law, and to **Israel for an everlasting covenant**, Saying, Unto thee will I give the land of Canaan, **the lot of your inheritance**; When ye were but few, even a few, and strangers in it." (1 Chronicles 16:15-19 – KJV – emphasis mine).*

The bloodline of an individual matters because blood is the carrier of life (see Leviticus 17:11). It was on the basis of ancestral covenants that God showed the children of Israel mercy when they were in the land of their enemies.

"And yet for all that, when they be in the land of their enemies, I will not cast them away, neither will I abhor them,

*to destroy them utterly, and **to break my covenant with them**: for I am the Lord their God. But I will for their sakes **remember the covenant of their ancestors**, whom I brought forth out of the land of Egypt in the sight of the heathen, that I might be their God: I am the Lord." (Leviticus 26:44-45 – KJV – emphasis mine).*

While covenants are housed within blood, science explains that blood cells are formed within the bone marrow. Thus, the bone is the source of ancestral blessings and curses. Jacob was a righteous man and understood that bones are not ordinary. In his last moments alive, he charged his sons to bury him with his fathers as opposed to leaving him (which in essence would be his remains, i.e., his bones) in Egypt (see Genesis 49:29). His son must have taken note because later in his dying days he made a similar request.

*"And **Joseph took an oath** of the children of Israel, saying, God will surely visit you, and **ye shall carry up my bones from hence.**" (Genesis 50:25 – KJV – emphasis mine).*

*"And Moses took the bones of Joseph with him: for he had **straitly sworn** the children of Israel, saying, God will surely visit you; and **ye shall carry up my bones away hence with you.**" (Exodus 13:19 – KJV – emphasis mine).*

***"And the bones of Joseph**, which the children of Israel brought up out of Egypt, buried they in Shechem, in a parcel of ground which Jacob bought of the sons of Hamor the father of Shechem for an hundred pieces of silver: and it* *became the inheritance of the children of Joseph." (Joshua 24:32 – KJV - emphasis mine).*

Joseph was intentional in instructing the Israelites on where his bones were to be buried, but the question is why? It is key to understand that because bones are spiritual houses of both blessings and curses, Joseph knew that once his bones remained in Egypt, the nation would have been blessed. Thus, for his bones' sake, i.e., the covenant God made with him through his father, Abraham, the land of Egypt would not have been judged because of a righteous man (see Genesis 18:23 and Ezekiel 22:30). Furthermore, the bones of a man not only acts as an intercessor but can give life as was the case of Elisha's.

*"And Elisha died, and they buried him. And the bands of the Moabites invaded the land at the coming in of the year. And it came to pass, **as they were burying a man**, that, behold, they spied a band of men; and they cast the **man into the sepulchre of Elisha**: and **when the man was let down, and touched the bones of Elisha, he revived, and stood up on his feet.**" (2 Kings 13:20-21 – KJV – emphasis mine).*

Whereas the bones of a righteous man can convey life and blessings, the bones of the wicked do the exact opposite.

*"**His bones are full of the sin of his youth**, which shall lie down with him in the dust." (Job 20:11 – KJV – emphasis mine).*

69

The above Scripture highlights a few key points. Firstly, one should be mindful of how he lives his life in his youth because the consequences of his actions will follow his bloodline beyond the grave. Another point is that the dust bears the record of man's ancestry. Consider why Jesus wrote in the dust (see John 8:6) or why the earth (in addition to the heaven) were called to bear record against the Israelites (see Deuteronomy 30:19). However, the main focus of this section is the bones. Have you ever taken note of the symbol that is used to identify those in the occult? It is that of skull and bones.

*"And they shall not lie with the mighty that are fallen of the uncircumcised, which are gone down to hell with their weapons of war: and they have laid their swords under their heads, but **their iniquities shall be upon their bones**, though they were the terror of the mighty in the land of the living." (Ezekiel 32:27 – KJV – emphasis mine).*

Have you ever noticed that those who are involved in witchcraft practices seem to age because their covenant is with darkness and death?

"Your covenant with death *will be annulled, and* **your agreement with Sheol** *will not stand; when the overflowing scourge passes through, then you will be trampled down by it." (Isaiah 28:18 – NKJV – emphasis mine).*

Without knowledge and understanding, the righteous becomes a prey by encountering untimely deaths, while the wicked live on (see Job's lamentation in Job 21:7). Josiah, being a wise young man, knew the spiritual implications of strange altars as well as their covenants which were hidden in bones.

*"Josiah was eight years old when he began to reign, and he reigned in Jerusalem one and thirty years. And he did that which was right in the sight of the Lord, and walked in the ways of David his father, and declined neither to the right hand, nor to the left. For in the eighth year of his reign, while he was yet young, he began to seek after the God of David his father: and in the twelfth year **he began to purge Judah and Jerusalem from the high places**, and the groves, and the carved images, and the molten images. **And they brake down the altars of Baalim** in his presence; and the images, that were on high above them, he cut down; and the groves, and the carved images, and the molten images, he brake in pieces, and made dust of them, and strowed it upon the graves of them that had sacrificed unto them. **And he burnt the bones of the priests upon their altars**, and **cleansed Judah and Jerusalem**." (2 Chronicles 34:1-5 – KJV – emphasis mine).*

To attract the blessings of God in his reign, King Josiah purged the land by burning the bones of the wicked priests. By burning the bones, Josiah was dismantling witchcraft from the roots (see Matthew 15:13). Fire was involved in this prophetic act because it is an instrument of judgment (see Revelation 8:5) and is used to refine and purge.

*"But who may abide the day of his coming? and who shall stand when he appeareth? For he is like a **refiner's fire, and like fullers' soap.**" (Malachi 3:2 – KJV – emphasis mine).*

*"Then flew one of the seraphims unto me, having **a live coal** in his hand, which he had taken with the tongs **from off the altar**: And he laid it upon my mouth, and said, Lo, this hath touched thy lips; and **thine iniquity is taken away, and thy sin purged.**" (Isaiah 6:6-7 – KJV – emphasis mine).*

The Covenant of Rest For The Land

As aforementioned, the earth, in more ways than one, is portrayed in the similitude of a woman. They both carry water and bring forth seed. Additionally, the woman experiences a natural sabbath when on her menstrual cycle. For that reason, during her cycle, she should not engage in strenuous activities. Similarly, the earth has a sabbath that the Lord, by covenant, has ordained that it should observe.

*"And the Lord spoke to Moses on Mount Sinai, saying, "Speak to the children of Israel, and say to them: 'When you come into the land which I give you, then **the land shall keep a sabbath to the Lord**. Six years you shall sow your field, and six years you shall prune your vineyard, and gather its fruit; but in the seventh year there shall be **a sabbath of solemn rest for the land, a sabbath to the Lord**. You shall neither sow your field nor prune your vineyard. What grows of its own accord of your harvest you shall not reap, nor gather the grapes of your untended*

*vine, **for it is a year of rest for the land**." (Leviticus 25:1-5 – NKJV – emphasis mine).*

The sabbath is not just a day but a gate, as well as a year, place, jubilee, and house. It is a secret place of intimacy where God meets with His own. In Genesis, Adam had constant communion with God, but after this intimacy was broken, not only was Adam separated from this house of rest, but the earth was placed in bondage (see Genesis 3:17,23).

When the children of Israel disobeyed this law of giving the land its rest, God's judgment was that of seventy years of captivity for the Israelites (see Daniel 9:2, 2 Chronicles 36:21, and Jeremiah 25:11). Likewise, if you own a farm, it is imperative that you observe the law of the sabbath so the blessings of God can remain upon you and your produce. The below Scripture further expounds on this:

*"'Then **the land shall enjoy its sabbaths as long as it lies desolate** and you are in your enemies' land; then **the land shall rest and enjoy its sabbaths**. As long as it lies desolate it shall rest—for the time it did not rest on your sabbaths when you dwelt in it." (Leviticus 26:34-35 – NKJV – emphasis mine).*

From the beginning of time, God outlined the pattern of working and resting for man to follow. However, this law was not limited to humans only, but God had the earth in mind as well.

*"Then I will remember My covenant with Jacob, and My covenant with Isaac and My covenant with Abraham I will remember; **I will remember the land**. The land also shall be left empty by them, and will enjoy its sabbaths while it lies desolate without them; they will accept their guilt, because they despised My judgments and because their soul abhorred My statutes." (Leviticus 26:42-43 – NKJV – emphasis mine).*

A land therefore can either receive the blessings of God if the inhabitants are obedient or incur the judgment of God through disobedience (see Leviticus 26). In the beginning, God's covenant with the earth and the whole of creation was one of rest and blessing. Thus, when violence begins to run rampant in the land, the land—being a living being—will respond.

*"**How long will the land mourn**, And the herbs of every field wither? The beasts and birds are consumed, for the wickedness of those who dwell there, because they said, "He will not see our final end."" (Jeremiah 12:4 – NKJV – emphasis mine).*

*"**Therefore the land will mourn**; and everyone who dwells there will waste away with the beasts of the field and the birds of the air; even the fish of the sea will be taken away." (Hosea 4:3 – NKJV – emphasis mine).*

*"For we know that **the whole creation groans and labors** with birth pangs together until now." (Romans 8:22 – NKJV – emphasis mine).*

The Altar Of The Land

It is imperative to reemphasize that every nation is governed by a covenant, and wherever there is a covenant, an altar is present. Though altars of righteousness do exist, the opposite is true. The troubles (inclusive of prostitution, murders, rapes and other heinous crimes) that a nation encounters are influenced by the mistress of witchcrafts (also called Mystery Babylon—see Revelation 17:5) whose covenant is with the waters.

*"Woe to the **bloody city**! it is all full of lies and robbery; the prey departeth not; The noise of a whip, and the noise of the rattling of the wheels, and of the pransing horses, and of the jumping chariots. The horseman lifteth up both the bright sword and the glittering spear: and there is a **multitude of slain**, and a **great number of carcases**; and there is none end of their corpses; they stumble upon their corpses: Because of the **multitude of the whoredoms of the wellfavoured harlot, the mistress of witchcrafts, that selleth nations through her whoredoms, and families through her witchcrafts**." (Nahum 3:1-4 – KJV – emphasis mine).*

This was the source of Pharaoh's power, which is why God judged him and his army in the Red Sea (see Exodus 15:3).

This further explains why God judged the waters by turning it into blood as one of the ten plagues (see Exodus 7:14-21). God dealt severely with Pharaoh because he was Satan himself, the great dragon (see Revelation 12:9). Let us look at the following Scripture:

*In the tenth year, in the tenth month, in the twelfth day of the month, the word of the Lord came unto me, saying, Son of man, **set thy face against Pharaoh king of Egypt, and prophesy against him**, and against all Egypt: Speak, and say, Thus saith the Lord God; Behold, I am against thee, **Pharaoh king of Egypt, the great dragon that lieth in the midst of his rivers, which hath said, My river is mine own, and I have made it for myself.** (Ezekiel 29:1-3 – NKJV – emphasis mine).*

Though he appeared to be a man, Pharaoh was actually a spirit. Many of our world's leaders have their covenant with the waters and, as such, the spirit responsible for the government of this age is from the waters. Thus, though they may have human forms, they are actually evil spirits whose covenant is with darkness so as to perpetuate evils in our societies.

*"Daniel spoke, saying, "I saw in my vision by night, and behold, the four winds of heaven were stirring up the Great Sea. And **four great beasts came up from the sea**, each different from the other. The first was like a lion, and had eagle's wings. I watched till its wings were plucked off; and it was lifted up from the earth and made to stand on two feet*

*like a man, **and a man's heart was given to it**." (Daniel 7:2-5 – NKJV – emphasis mine).*

Water is not innocent because not only is it a witness on the earth (see 1 John 5:8) but it is an ancient, i.e., water preexisted before creation and was not a part of God's agenda (see Genesis 1:1-2). Not only is there a government on land but also one in the sea (see Nahum 2:6). With this understanding, therefore, the blood of the Lamb must be invoked to speak against the strange altars ruling our nations because all creation—including the waters—are upheld by the blood that was shed from the foundation of the world (see Revelation 13:8 and Psalm 24:1-2).

Chapter 8
How Do We Approach The Altar

D avid, in Psalm 24, gives us a clear indication on how to approach the altar:

"He that hath clean hands, and a pure heart; who hath not lifted up his soul unto vanity, nor sworn deceitfully." (Psalm 24:4 - KJV).

He who is innocent of hands and pure of heart, who does not lift up his soul to falseness, and does not swear deceitfully. (Psalm 24:4 - LEM[8]).

Enduring Word Bible Commentary by David GUZIK gives us a good exposition of this verse:

a) **He who has clean hands and a pure heart**: This speaks of a man or woman who is pure in both their actions (**hands**) and intentions (**heart**). This one can *ascend the hill of the LORD* and *stand in His holy place.*

     i.   David already established that God ruled the earth; now he declared that God rules the

---

[8] Lexham English Bible

earth on a *moral* foundation. He is concerned with the moral behavior of mankind.

    ii.   **Clean hands** are important for good hygiene, but this speaks of much more than washing with water. Pontius Pilate washed his hands, but they were not clean.

    iii.   "But *'clean hands'* would not suffice, unless they were connected with *'a pure heart.'* True religion is heart-work."[9]

b) **Who has not lifted up his soul to an idol**: The one accepted by God also rejects idolatry in his actions and especially in his **soul**.

    iv.   "The meaning of *lift up his soul* is illuminated by Psalm 25:1, where it is parallel to 'trust'."[10]

c) **Nor sworn deceitfully:** The words we speak are a good indication of the state of our hearts, the inner man or woman (see Matthew 12:34). One who makes deceptive promises finds no welcome from God.

    v.   David understood all this under the general principles of the Old Covenant, in which God promised to bless and receive obedient Israel,

---

[9] Spurgeon
[10] Kidner

and also promised to curse and afflict a disobedient Israel (see <u>Deuteronomy 27-28</u>).

vi.   Outside the terms of the Old Covenant that God made with Israel, these answers of David may cause one to despair. It is easy to look at this list and see that my hands are not always clean; my heart is not always pure. Idolatry can be both subtle and stubborn in my heart. I also find it too easy to make promises with at least a tinge of deceit.

vii.   Fortunately, God established a better covenant, a New Covenant through the person and work of Jesus. Under the New Covenant, we see that Jesus is the one **who has clean hands and a pure heart,** perfectly so. Jesus has *never* **lifted up his soul to an idol**, and has *never* **sworn deceitfully**.

In *His* righteousness, given to all who believe (see <u>Romans 3:22</u>), we can ascend His holy hill and stand in His holy place.

viii.   "Our Lord Jesus Christ could ascend into the hill of the Lord because His hands were clean and His heart was pure, and if we by faith in Him are conformed to His image we shall enter too."[11]

---

[11] Spurgeon

ix.   Nevertheless, David's principle is also accurate under the New Covenant in this sense: the conduct of one's life is a reflection of his fellowship with God. As John wrote: *If we say that we have fellowship with Him, and walk in darkness, we lie and do not practice the truth* (1 John 1:6). We might say that under the Old Covenant, a righteous walk was the *precondition* for fellowship with God; under the New Covenant, a righteous walk is the *result* of fellowship with God, founded on faith. Yet under both covenants, God cares very much about the moral conduct of mankind, especially those who identify themselves as His people.

Remember, we cannot hide our inner thoughts from God, so open up and express yourself to Him in the fear of the Lord, knowing that you are covered by the blood of Jesus on the cross over two thousand years ago. The blood is still speaking and will never stop speaking on our behalf, and you are before a loving God.

Chapter 9
Fuel on the Altar

As a boy growing up on the island of Jamaica, we did not have gas or electric stove. What we had was a woodfire, and to keep the fire burning, we constantly had to put wood in the fire. We always had to stock up on dry wood, and as the wood burnt out, we replenished the fire with more wood.

Christians must ensure that the fire on their altar is never burnt out by constantly and consistently keeping in prayer. As discussed in previous chapters, it is our prayer that keeps the altar going; our altar is serviced by prayer; it is the fuel that keeps the altar alive. Prayer opens up a portal in the heavens for God to come and operate on the earth.

Now when all the people were baptized, it came to pass, that Jesus also being baptized, and praying, the heaven was opened, and the Holy Ghost descended in a bodily shape like a dove upon him, and a voice came from heaven, which said, Thou art my beloved Son; in thee I am well pleased. (Luke 3:21-22 – KJV).

Note carefully it was the prayer of Jesus that opened the heaven and that divine encounter took place. He was empowered to go into the wilderness in prayer and fasting, and He was victorious over the temptation put to Him by the devil.

There are five things that happens when we pray:

1. Communion and fellowship

Prayer is one of the ways we have communion and fellowship with God; prayer is sanctioned by God. It is God giving us permission to communicate with Him on a personal basis through His Son, Jesus Christ. A prayerless Christian life means there is no communion and fellowship with God.

And it came to pass in those days, that he went out into a mountain to pray, and continued all night in prayer to God. (Luke 6:12 – KJV).

Then cometh Jesus with them unto a place called Gethsemane, and saith unto the disciples, Sit ye here, while I go and pray yonder. (Matthew 26:36 – KJV).

Jesus, the Son of God, had to be in constant communion and fellowship with God, the Father, and we must follow the life of Jesus. In Luke 6, Jesus spent all night in prayer before He chose the twelve disciples.

2. Transformation

The more we pray, the more we are transformed into the image and likeness of Christ. Transformation is an inner change that is expressed outwardly. The Greek word for transformed, according to Romans 12:2, has the meaning of **being changed into another form**. It is a total change for the better.

Therefore if any man be in Christ, he is a new creature: old things are passed away; behold, all things are become new. (2 Corinthians 5:17 – KJV).

For transformation to take place in the life of Jacob, he had to spend the entire night in prayer. His prayer opened the heaven that led to an encounter with an angel from heaven, which brought about a name change and a character change. Jacob was no more Jacob the supplanter or deceiver but Israel.

And he said, Thy name shall be called no more Jacob, but Israel: for as a prince hast thou power with God and with men, and hast prevailed. (Genesis 32:28 – KJV).

What are your struggles? What are those bad habits in your life? What are you battling with? Are you still being controlled by the flesh? Are you still pursuing the things of the world? Unless one is being transformed by the Holy Spirit, all these will lead one into temptation and to one yielding to temptation.

Be a Jacob and spend sufficient time in prayer. Do not leave the altar until your <u>all</u> is laid there; total transformation is guaranteed to take place through the power of the Holy Ghost with fervency in prayer.

"As we spend time praying, reading the word, focusing on God, worshiping him in spirit and in truth, our thought process will respond in a positive manner. You will begin to desire to grow spiritually. As your spirit is refreshed by the Holy Spirit, you will grow stronger in faith. The word of God is a type of spiritual water that will refresh your soul. Spiritual dryness will be replaced with new growth in your spirit. Just as plants are refreshed by the rain, you will be refreshed by the Holy Spirit as he enlightens the truth of the scriptures to your heart and mind.

A healthy lifestyle will replace the unhealthy lifestyle and you will begin to flourish spiritually. You will be transformed.

God desires that we not just have the word of God near us, but in us. In our minds, in our hearts, and allowing the Holy Spirit to apply the word to our hearts and work in our lives. The Holy Spirit makes alive the word of God in our hearts, and that will produce a transformation in our lives. The transformation that Paul is referring to in Romans 12 and other places in scripture will only happen if we allow it, and say yes to Jesus." [12]

---

[12] Pastor Richard Rogers – Life is a Journey, Part 30, How to live a transformed life.

3. Your will dies, and you take on the will of God

The will is that faculty of the mind by which we determine either to do or forbear an action; the faculty used in deciding, among two or more objects, which we shall embrace or pursue. The will is directed or influenced by the judgment. The understanding or reason compares different objects, which operate as motives; the judgment determines which is preferable, and the will decides which to pursue. In other words, we reason with respect to the value or importance of things; we then judge which is to be preferred; and we will to take the most valuable. These are but different operations of the mind, soul, or intellectual part of man.[13]

Through prayer and the power of the Holy Spirit, one will be given the power to bring under control one's actions, emotions and desires in accordance with the Word of God. In prayer, one will make meaningful and right choices. One now takes on the will of God; one can declare "What God wants, I want. God's ways are my ways." When we take on the will of God, we can safely say as the Apostle Paul in 1 Corinthians 11:1, "Be ye followers of me, even as I also *am* of Christ."

Jesus took on the will of God at the greatest and most challenging time in His life, nearing the great suffering He was going to undergo. Jesus had to surrender His will to the will of God.

---

[13] KJV Dictionary Definition

Saying, Father, if thou be willing, remove this cup from me: nevertheless not my will, but thine, be done. And there appeared an angel unto him from heaven, strengthening him. And being in an agony he prayed more earnestly: and his sweat was as it were great drops of blood falling down to the ground. And when he rose up from prayer, and was come to his disciples, he found them sleeping for sorrow. (Luke 22:42-45 – KJV).

Let us take on the will of God for our lives.

Here are a few scriptures to meditate on as you seek earnestly in prayer to be walking, living, and abiding in the will of God.

Trust in the LORD with all thine heart; and lean not unto thine own understanding. (Proverbs 3:5 – KJV).

For as many as are led by the Spirit of God, they are the sons of God. (Romans 8:14).

For we are his workmanship, created in Christ Jesus unto good works, which God hath before ordained that we should walk in them. (Ephesians 2:10 – KJV).

I beseech you therefore, brethren, by the mercies of God, that ye present your bodies a living sacrifice, holy, acceptable unto God, which is your reasonable service. And be not conformed to this world: but be ye transformed by the renewing of your mind, that ye may prove what is that good,

*and acceptable, and perfect, will of God. (Romans 12:1-2 –
KJV).*

4. A deep desire for the things of God

Valuable time spent at the altar will give you a deep desire
for the things of God. Growth of body, soul, and spirit will
take place, which will lead to fellowship with God and man.

With this greater desire for God and the things of God, we
will seek to build His Kingdom and make a meaningful and
powerful impact on this world. There is absolutely more to
God than what we are experiencing on a daily basis, and God
wants to reveal more of His glory to us, but only when we
come after Him with all our hearts.

In this world, people are hungry and thirsty for power,
prestige, fame, and wealth, but God is seeking a people who
is thirsty for Him, the living God. God will only manifest
His fullness and His glory to those who earnestly seek after
Him at the altar of prayer. Let us develop that hunger and
thirst and a deep desire for the things of God.

Our main desires should not be focused on our success,
comfort, safety or health, but a strong zeal for the glory,
presence, and radiance of God to be experienced and seen in
our lives daily as we walk and experience His goodness each
day.

O God, thou art my God; early will I seek thee: my soul thirsteth for thee, my flesh longeth for thee in a dry and thirsty land, where no water is; To see thy power and thy glory, so as I have seen thee in the sanctuary. (Psalm 63:1-2 – KJV).

Ho, every one that thirsteth, come ye to the waters, and he that hath no money; come ye, buy, and eat; yea, come, buy wine and milk without money and without price. (Isaiah 55:1 – KJV).

As the hart panteth after the water brooks, so panteth my soul after thee, O God. My soul thirsteth for God, for the living God: when shall I come and appear before God? (Psalm 42:1-2 – KJV).

Blessed are they which do hunger and thirst after righteousness: for they shall be filled. (Matthew 5:6 – KJV).

5. One with the Father

The major goal, or one of the keys of prayer, is oneness with God, the Father. Prayer is much more than asking for needs to be met. It is coming into oneness with the Father, taking on the divine nature of the Father.

Oneness with the Father means I think like Him, act like Him, walk like Him, live like Him, love like Him, and forgive like Him.

Oneness with the Father will lead us to operate in the supernatural—that which is above and beyond nature—walking and operating in the miraculous power of God. Only when we are one with the Father can we operate in signs and wonders on the earth, for the Father will approve of us.

Ye men of Israel, hear these words; Jesus of Nazareth, a man approved of God among you by miracles and wonders and signs, which God did by him in the midst of you, as ye yourselves also know: (Acts 2:22 – KJV).

Jesus' ministry shows oneness with God, the Father, and we should all follow the life of Jesus, our Lord and Saviour.

I and my Father are one. (John 10:30 – KJV).

But if I do, though ye believe not me, believe the works: that ye may know, and believe, that the Father is in me, and I in him. (John 10:38 – KJV).

Believest thou not that I am in the Father, and the Father in me? the words that I speak unto you I speak not of myself: but the Father that dwelleth in me, he doeth the works. Believe me that I am in the Father, and the Father in me: or else believe me for the very works' sake. Verily, verily, I say unto you, He that believeth on me, the works that I do shall he do also; and greater works than these shall he do; because I go unto my Father. (John 14:10-12 – KJV).

And now I am no more in the world, but these are in the world, and I come to thee. Holy Father, keep through thine own name those whom thou hast given me, that they may be one, as we are. (John 17:11 – KJV).

And the glory which thou gavest me I have given them; that they may be one, even as we are one: I in them, and thou in me, that they may be made perfect in one; and that the world may know that thou hast sent me, and hast loved them, as thou hast loved me. (John 17:22-23 – KJV).

The Secret Place

Let us now find that secret place, that meeting place with God, the Father; this is our quiet and personal time with God.

The secret place is our training ground, our time of knowing the voice of God, and developing a deep intimacy with GOD. It is us digging wells by ourselves to get into the depths of God where we can be fed and drink from the well of living water so we thirst no more.

In the secret place, the Holy Spirit is totally in charge, we are built up in Christ, growth takes place, and we come to know the will of GOD.

But thou, when thou prayest, enter into thy closet, and when thou hast shut thy door, pray to thy Father which is in secret; and thy Father which seeth in secret shall reward thee openly. (Matthew 6:6 – KJV).

What the Bible refers to as the "secret place" is where you get alone with God and spend time in fellowship with Him. The secret place is any private place; it could be an office, your house, bedroom, or closet. It is wherever you are alone with God. It is the place where you experience God's manifested presence, where you encounter all that He is in order that you may reveal His glory and power to others. In the overflow of His presence, favor and supernatural power come as a result. The depth of your hunger will lead to the greatest depths of His presence in your life.

Conclusion

The use of altars is dated from the beginning of time and, hence, documented in the book of Genesis. We see altar building, its uses and significance starting with Abraham (Father Abraham). The biblical significance of altars continued throughout the lineage of Abraham and is no different for us today.

We see how the altar was used to capture Christ/God's attention, especially in times of needs—trouble or situations which seemed impossible to the natural man. Therefore, the essentiality of having an altar to approach the Lord cannot be overemphasized. As we practice this, we experience results that are often dumbfounded testimonies.

One must not forget, however, that there is a sacrificial aspect to the working of the altar, and since we don't slay animals anymore, then the sacrifice must be ourselves. Our hearts must be pure, our lives must reflect that of Christ, and we must be willing to put those things aside which would hinder the answer of God on our altar.

As you have read this book, it is my desire that you begin to experience the awesome presence of the Lord at your altar—that God meets you and the smoke of His glory engulfs you whenever you approach your altar.

Let me urge my readers who are not servicing their altars to begin doing so, remembering that your altar should not be a selfish place but one where intercession is done for your church, family, country, and world.

In closing, my brothers and sisters, I declare there is **power** at your righteous altar; there is **deliverance** at your righteous altar; there is **healing and breakthrough** at your righteous altar.

God is waiting to encounter you at your righteous altar today.

About the Author

Roderick Senior holds a doctorate in biblical counselling, masters degree in pastoral counselling, a bachelor's degree in theology, a diploma in principles and practices of supervision, and a certificate in principles and techniques of counselling. He also obtained a certificate in accounting from the Association of Accounting Technician (A.A.T).

He became a member of the Church of God of Prophecy in the year 1984. He currently serves as Parish Supervisor for eighteen local churches in St. Catherine West, Jamaica, and he is the pastor for two of these congregations. He is also a licensed Marriage Officer for the island of Jamaica.

He is married to Cheryl for over thirty years. They have two sons: Jhavel and Javon.

Roderick Senior describes his God-given mandate as that of touching lives in a positive way, playing his part in leading people to Jesus and helping them transform into "the image and likeness of our Lord and Saviour, Jesus Christ."

Power of the Altar Scriptures

A few scriptures to highlight the power of the altar:

Genesis 8:20-22

And Noah builded an altar unto the LORD; and took of every clean beast, and of every clean fowl, and offered burnt offerings on the altar. And the LORD smelled a sweet savour; and the LORD said in his heart, I will not again curse the ground any more for man's sake; for the imagination of man's heart is evil from his youth; neither will I again smite any more every thing living, as I have done. While the earth remaineth, seedtime and harvest, and cold and heat, and summer and winter, and day and night shall not cease. (KJV).

Genesis 12:7-8

And the LORD appeared unto Abram, and said, Unto thy seed will I give this land: and there builded he an altar unto the LORD, who appeared unto him. And he removed from thence unto a mountain on the east of Bethel, and pitched his tent, having Bethel on the west, and Hai on the east: and there he builded an altar unto the LORD, and called upon the name of the LORD. (KJV).

Genesis 13:3-4

And he went on his journeys from the south even to Bethel, unto the place where his tent had been at the beginning, between Bethel and Hai; Unto the place of the altar, which he had made there at the first: and there Abram called on the name of the LORD. (KJV).

Ephesians 6:18
Praying always with all prayer and supplication in the Spirit, and watching thereunto with all perseverance and supplication for all saints; (KJV).

1 Peter 3:12
For the eyes of the Lord are over the righteous, and his ears are open unto their prayers: but the face of the Lord is against them that do evil. (KJV).

Matthew 21:21-22
Jesus answered and said unto them, Verily I say unto you, If ye have faith, and doubt not, ye shall not only do this which is done to the fig tree, but also if ye shall say unto this mountain, Be thou removed, and be thou cast into the sea; it shall be done. And all things, whatsoever ye shall ask in prayer, believing, ye shall receive. (KJV).

2 Chronicles 7:14
If my people, which are called by my name, shall humble themselves, and pray, and seek my face, and turn from their wicked ways; then will I hear from heaven, and will forgive their sin, and will heal their land. (KJV).